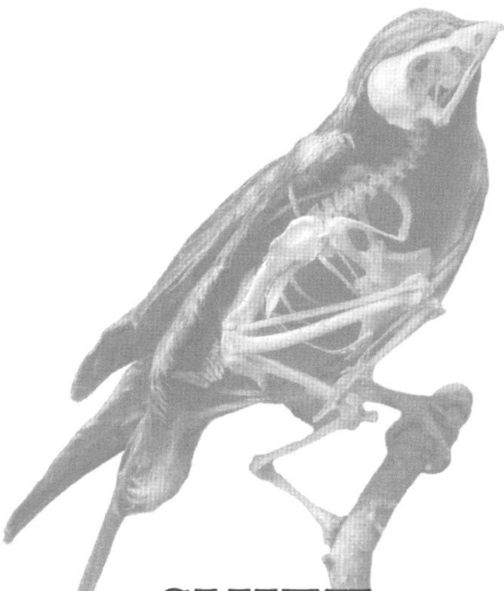

SHIFT

SHIFT

KELLY SHEPHERD

thistledown press

Thistledown Press Ltd.
410 2nd Avenue North
Saskatoon, Saskatchewan, S7K 2C3
www.thistledownpress.com

Library and Archives Canada Cataloguing in Publication

Shepherd, Kelly, 1974-, author
Shift / Kelly Shepherd.

Poems.
ISBN 978-1-77187-104-4 (paperback)
I. Title.

PS8637.H4765S55 2016 C811'.6 C2016-901048-1

Author photo: Randall Edwards
Cover and book design by Jackie Forrie
Printed and bound in Canada

Canada Council for the Arts Conseil des Arts du Canada

Saskatchewan Arts Board

Canada

Thistledown Press gratefully acknowledges the financial assistance of the Canada Council for the Arts, the Saskatchewan Arts Board, and the Government of Canada through the Canada Book Fund for its publishing program.

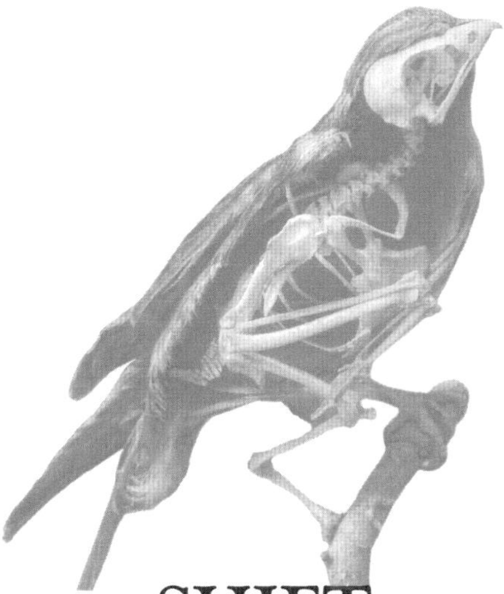

SHIFT

Contents

For my grandparents:
Doreen Helen Mosley, née Pease
Wilfred Benjamin Mosley
Marjorie Esther May Shepherd, née Charlton
Stanley John Shepherd

Honing

Your job is to take the cement —
grey-green, ugly, utilitarian, dusty and not just dusty but
poisonous, abrasive, blocky, sharp-edged, impossibly heavy
and dangerous in slings from overheard lifts —
and transform it into something else.

Pull off the present disk,
fingers fat with heavy rubber gloves,
and whack the grinder wheel's Velcro pad
down onto the next one waiting;
change again as the cement becomes smoother,
to a finer grade. The finishing disk is soft as felt —
you can almost believe this wouldn't hurt your skin —
but still the grinder doesn't get any lighter, the grip
can't loosen or falter, the cement-dust water
keeps splashing and spraying off the surface.

You're wearing an apron that reaches your ankles,
boots that reach your knees,
gloves that begin at your shoulders, as well as
eye, ear, and head protection:
peripheral vision and bodily sensations are limited,
fingers and body and senses are numb.
Water hitting the rubber feels muffled,
not quite related to you, same as the sound reaching your ears.
It's a busy cement plant, there are workers all around you,
but you're alone.

In two weeks a dozen cement surfaces
will be as smooth as glass to the fingers,
and speckled like a river full of colourful stones:
as if by grinding away the cement that encases them
you've returned the pebbles in the cement-mix gravel
to their rightful place, to their proper status as beautiful things.
Somewhere in the deadening noise and the grimy damp,

with hurting hands and dripping hardhat
there is a precise moment. The cement has revealed itself to you.
Somewhere between the second and third abrasive disk,
you see it open itself up and
the stones glimmer like stars in a night sky.

Other people, your co-workers and employers,
see the finished product only after it dries:
they run their hands over it admiringly, then
wipe the fine dust on their legs,
but they don't see it when it really shines.

In two weeks there will be an injury in your right hand,
so many hours with the same rigid grip, the same position,
you won't be able to straighten your fingers.
But you'll forget that. Your hands will loosen and recover.
You'll forget what you ate for lunch every day, and
what people talked about in the lunchroom.
The comments and faces of the dusty unsmiling workers will fade.
You'll forget the early morning bus rides to work, and
the exhausted evening rides home.
With years and repetition all the tasks, machine noises,
coffee cups, and even people start to blur.
Days of this employment become like water hitting a rubber suit.
Almost, you'll forget this particular job entirely.

Tire Song

I am the moment between metal
and air that makes speed possible.

My life's purpose is to turn in
circles so that you can go straight.

I sing landscape left
behind and places reduced to space.

I am earth rammed
through tubes; I shout dark explosions.

I am efficiency's triumph over gravity.
My runes are friction-trails of snakes.

My life is shorter than my death.
I am the colour the sky turns when I burn.

Webs Across the Eyes

Some spiders know the knots
to tie a cluster of Oregon grape
into one single dusty purple berry. If a

black bear swallows it under the right moon
he or she will become a powerful shaman,
able to speak the language of spiders. Such a

bear knows the secret
of setting intricate snares, moving quietly,
and avoiding all but the most blessed of human beings.

Knell for the Canary

don't be afraid of the dark
          (be afraid of the dark)

your owners will watch out for you
          (watch out, watch out)

even when they're not near you
          (they're not near you)

even when you sing alone
          (you sing alone)

far from the ringing of picks and shovels
          (ringing, ringing)

Drum-riding

Grasshoppers spend the night
between the roof and the fly,
wait out the cold and wet;
gone by late morning.

The tent is a boat
drum-taut in wind,
a skin kayak in waves,
afloat on a grass sea.

Under the rain the tent is a drum:
light rain the grasshoppers
finding their places to sleep;
heavy rain the horses
as we ride it into the sky.

Odd

There are ninety-nine names of Allah; he who commits them to memory would get into Paradise. Verily, Allah is Odd (He is one, and it is an odd number) and He loves odd numbers.

— Muslim ibn al-Hajjaj Nishapuri, *Sahih Muslim*

With his tail the squirrel ratchets himself up the tree.
Then noisily — sometimes angrily, it appears to us —
the squirrel prostrates himself on the branch.

The squirrel has found the pine cones inscribed
with ninety-eight of the ninety-nine names of God.
He has not yet found the cone that bears

the ninety-ninth name. He is still looking.
He cannot rest. Between searches the squirrel will select
one or sometimes three of the ninety-eight names

he has taken all this time
to gather, and conceal them deep in the forest.
To our eyes this is a purely random act;

we wonder if the squirrel is sane.
He hides the names of God from himself
and all the while he searches.

Poor Henry David Thoreau (found)

Thank God,
men can
not as yet fly,
and lay
waste the sky
as well as
the earth!

We are safe
on that side
for the present.

(*Journal*, 3 January 1861)

In Exchange for Flight

Falling, a cat lands on its feet
only by relaxing its muscles,
surrendering to the air

while a bird hollows its bones,
letting the sky enter its body
in exchange for flight.

For a man in dark water
any light,
any horizon will do.

If his hands are like
the hands of a clock,
he will drown at midnight.

It is time. The man sinks.
The water is not aware
the man does not know he is water.

The Fire

Smoke-sniffle sap-dotted palms smoky shirt
O the day after an evening fire.

O the fire:
entranced by this living bright hot

crackle dark orange dance of wood,
we always sit too close.

The rising sparks
like prayers

the waves of heat on our faces,
answers.

To Make Tea

we boiled stinging-nettle shoots and powdery dandelion flowers
in cold water tasting of smooth rocks and pine needles carried down
the road in blue plastic pails from Gramophone Creek, nettles and
dandelions from the garden growing all around the garden fence

Breathing the liquor-sweet earth-scent of dark
berries in an old green tent in the late August sun, mildewy
canvas, old sleeping bags, tongue-lolling dogs, tent-flaps wide open to
and sleeping bags barely containing and dogs rolling river-wet in
the summertime poplar-sap fresh-turned soil evening
hayfields wood smoke and Saskatoon tea

Yellowhead Tamaracks

Driving 16,
Edmonton through Jasper,
and then opting
for the south, perhaps,
for Kamloops in
-stead of Prince George,

but before that
the October slopes
keep you right where
you are: forgetting
speed limits, trans
-fixed by the number

of trees which in
summer you'd dismissed
as evergreens, now
whole forests painted
by the same guys
who do the centre line.

Greyhound Night Song

The darkness is a grey-silver green that moves
in front of the eyes like dust.
It will be clear soon but here we are, not sure
which side of the sun we're on.
The windshield wipers push aside small bits
of lakes and clouds and the music on the radio small bits
of conversation coming from the back of the bus
but don't worry, everything
will get to where it's meant to go.

Ritual: To Find Out How Much Sunlight is Left (found)

face the sun, fully
extend your arms
towards the sun,
wrists bent inwards,
your fingers just
below the sun,
disregard
the thumbs.

Count how many finger widths
separate the sun from the horizon.
Allow fifteen minutes per finger.
If four fingers fill the space
between the horizon and the sun,
sunset is an hour away.

Eye of the Storm

There was the house, an old squared-log home built probably eighty or a hundred years ago, and there was the washboard gravel road. The rest was chaos tied tight with binder-twine.

Alvin Miller's yard could've been a museum, with its rusting farm equipment and dilapidated buildings. Red bantams and yellow dogs negotiated creaking wire gates, vintage tractors succumbing to Scottish thistles and fireweed under wind-shredded tarpaulins.

One big lean-to woodshed would have fallen long ago if the green 1950-something Chevrolet hadn't been backed up against the wall. All you'd need is a new motor, four new tires, and who knows what else: drive that truck away and the whole building would collapse in a heap. When you're eight or ten years old this doesn't occur to you.

And when Dad led one of Alvin's cows in from the blowing snow to give birth, that building was the shelter he chose. I was there; I leaned on the green truck's fender to watch.

There were complications. The calf wasn't budging. I remember its hooves sticking out from the back of the cow, pale and delicate. I remember melting snow and wet manure. My dad's hands kept slipping, with and without leather gloves. *Rope,* Alvin said, taking a tangle of yellow nylon from a nail on the wall. He held it between his chin and his chest while he opened a pocket knife.

This was the man who had built and repaired and rebuilt generations of machinery and outbuildings: Alvin Miller knew how to use tools. But on that day, maybe it was all the melting snow, his hand slipped when he tried to cut a short length of rope and the blade bit into the meat just below his thumb.

Alvin Miller, who had over the years single-handedly chopped the heads off of hundreds of chickens, who had slaughtered and butchered dozens of cows and pigs, and who had personally castrated dozens of young bulls, took one look at his own blood and pitched forward, face-first into the dirty hay, in a dead faint.

Come here, my dad said. *Hold this. Don't let the loop slip off.* And he handed me the rope.

Translucent

Soon the morning will climb
to the tops of the trees.
The cicada that I became
so that I might follow the sun
and sing away the memories
of dark larval stages,

so that I might tell the stories
of root-tips deep underground
to the new green branches
that sway high in the air

has turned into
a rust-coloured leaf.

The Omnivore’s Dilemma (found)

As I came home through the woods
with my string of fish, trailing my pole,

it being now quite dark,
I caught a glimpse
of a woodchuck stealing
across my path,

and felt a strange thrill
of savage delight,
and was strongly tempted
to seize and devour him raw;

not that I was hungry, then, except
for the wildness that he represented.

In the Grass

trying to stomp the serpent
back into the earth

you injure your heel: a puncture wound
from broken bison bones

Domestic

A quadruped with no knees, an animal so
thoroughly domesticated it doesn't
move. For hundreds of years its broad

shoulders and flat back have been used
for human work. It is long-lived and quiet,
and would be the perfect servant except

for one flaw: a rare congenital bone disease
in some individuals causes one leg to grow
shorter than the others, resulting in an

unstable rocking motion. This is especially
common among the smaller subspecies
found most often in coffee shops.

The Human Skin (found)

Ahimsa taken too literally
leaves out the life of the world
and makes the rabbit virtuous
but the hawk evil.

People who must fish
and hunt to live
can enter into the process
with gratitude and care,
and no arrogant assumptions
of human privilege.

This cannot come from
"thinking about" nature;
it must come from
being *within* nature.

Agelaius phoeniceus

I am the colour of the nest
because eggs are not
and I need to hide you
until you can fly.

Your father's shoulders
every father's shoulders
are marked with the colours
of the great bright bird in the sky
to remind them of what they do
every morning.

Nothing is more important.

When a water strider's pinlegs dimple
the reflection of a bird on pondwater
if that bird is not singing
that same night will bring an owl
before the moon.

If cattails in the wind sing more loudly
or more beautifully than evening birds
their nestlings will not know their true parents
and might choose to stay with the reeds
when the freeze comes.

Without our songs when once again
the great bird in the sky is learning to fly,
he might not leave the nest of night
and the day will not come.

Big Lake Poplars

If a cloud is lake speech
does a forest sing deer?

The water's body
is reinhydrated in air;

cloud reflects lake
the way antlers
rhyme with branches.

Breakneck

There was no time to take cameras
out of bags, so everyone
saw it but there was no evidence

later. After the trucks pulled over
at the trailhead, but before most
of us had stepped out onto the gravel

logging road, a cow moose ran past
wheezing and flecked with sweat. Her
calf, less than a year old, galloped

close behind. A hockey stick's length
from the truck, someone said. After
the calf came a light brown grizzly bear

also winded but running steadily. In
the dim spruce silence we could hear all
three of them breathing. It might be

a stretch to say the bear looked
confident but it seemed clear that the
end was near for the moose. The calf

would be the bear's obvious target
and the cow would die before she'd
let that happen. No time, no time

Smash

Wishing they could fly like
insects or birds humans
have built sky-coloured walls.

Butterflies hit their heads on flowers
and bees fly face-first into clover leaves
both already recoiling from bumping

slowly into stones underground;
swallows mistake bowls of soup
in restaurant windows for nests

and smash their beaks on the glass.
With hands and faces covered in bee stings
and teeth broken on stones

the diners look up from their meals.

Storm Birds

The tree is shaped like a cloud,
dark and wide across the sky, a pillar
cumulonimbus and shifting in the wind.

Near the centre of the cloud
is an oblong tangle of shadow and stillness,
a magpie's nest, the eye of the storm.

Winds which are magpies, their wings,
circle the cloud and change direction
abruptly to cut through it. Lightning, streaks

and bright feathers, interrupts the dark.
Thunderheads fill horizons
of telephone wires and rooftops.

Daylight is replaced with dark.
More magpie wind cuts through the branches,
More lightning, more feathers.

The eye
is not what we think it is. In the middle
of the cloud there is not one still black point,

but two. A great raven, more quietly thunderous
than the crow-clouds, is attacking the nest.
Oblivious to wind and lightning,

the raven pulls one stick and then another
from the centre of the storm,
and drops them like hailstones.

Magpies dive. The raven's power is not
in its thick wet beak or nimbostratus wings
but in its ability to ignore.

Inside the nest, the point of the storm,
is unborn wind and lightning that
will never illuminate the sky.

The Straight Lines of Cities

That man talking a little too loudly: look at his callused hands.
He bent for half a summer levelling, compacting a bed of gravel
and sand; for half a summer he flexed his wrists and calves fitting

cobblestones together. These are the cobblestones, this is the
sidewalk under our feet. Who walks her dog here, or rides his
bike, and thinks about the hands and the backs, the bent-axle

wheelbarrows and sweat-fogged safety glasses? Look at the corners,
where the blocks had to be measured and cut before they'd fit: he
damaged his hearing shaping those with a circular saw. I was there,

and so was he, when a young guy on our landscaping crew sheared
off his index finger with that same saw. His scream wasn't as loud as
the noise of that diamond-spinner, that brick-eater; so we watched

him yell but didn't know why he yelled, at first, couldn't hear him,
just watched him drop the block he was cutting and grip his
spurting hand to his chest. That man talking a little too loudly,

he shut the saw off. It was with those hands. He helped the guy
into the pickup; his face was just as pale and tight as his friend's,
but he drove him to the hospital. Sat with him, I was told, in the

emergency room. Someone wondered, before we started again on
that stretch of sidewalk, if the finger could be reattached. One
surface fitted up against the other. The saw pumped water onto its

blade, so there would be no dust; dirty water dripped back into the
reservoir, through a filter, back into the pipe to the blade. That
afternoon, like every afternoon, the circular saw washed itself

clean. Got muddy, washed itself again. What does a saw know about blood? We with earplugs and shaking hands, after that, worked through the noise of the screaming, pulsing thing, tried not

to think too much about it. Just to finish the sidewalk. That man talking a little too loudly, and the man whose hand was maimed, wherever he is now, all of us: that was just one summer. Just a job.

No one thinks about these things. And I'm sure no one could find the half-finished cobblestone, even if they knew, and even if they tried, the bloody one that was picked up from the grass and

sprayed clean, white-knuckled, and finally cut and fit into its place.

Myrmidon Gauntlet

Now

I pull away, shake and pick off
the ants. Even on the pale
soft skin between fingers

the bites aren't visible
but they make the eyes water
with their faint acid scent.

Just minutes earlier

the hill was simmering with red
ants before I took a scoop off the top,
boiling over with them after. Then

with a little boy's startled jump
and a man's self-control,
don't move your hand; with

a fierce grin not entirely boy
nor grown man as the crawling
black and red became a glove.

Water in Religious Symbolism

The sand on the lake bottom
is shaped more like water
than the water is.

Let's believe in that.

Big Lake Ranch, BC

The days were long and hot,
cottonwood-leaf sharp.
I remember my sunburned shoulders,
carrying water, and the wide
-brimmed hat and sunburned
calves of my brother
who walked in front of me
carrying water.
The days were long and bright
and beautiful as the sun on the lake,
the dipping buckets,
calling loons.

Window: "Wind's Eye"

driving all day, Edmonton to Kelowna

> in the morning wet snow hit the windshield and
> in the evening warm bugs but some
> where in between

there was a line we crossed
that was a border not between provinces

> but between early and late
> between cold sap and warm
> between leaves as mist and leaves in mist

there was a place in the mountains
there was a moment

> when the steering wheel started to bloom
> the seats sprouted and
> the windshield blinked in the sun

Little Thunderstorm Songs

Grasshopper,
your legs like lightning,
the rain is coming!
Find someplace to hide.

Dragonfly —
all your work!
The wind is rising,
the pond will burst its seams.

Fort McMurray Acrostic (found: public washroom)

So
You
Newfies
Can
Receive
Unemployment
Down
East

Airstrip

Buckle up! The twin-engine plane was loaded; the guy
with toque and beard who had been operating the forklift
climbed into the cockpit. *This is your captain speaking,*

he said with a grin, *and this is the only airline in Canada
where you're still allowed to smoke!* He lit a cigarette before
starting the engines. We labourers belted ourselves in

to seats bolted to the cold metal walls of the cargo hold.
Up front there was the pilot, the co-pilot, and a tall, tanned
young woman with platinum-blonde hair down to her

waist. Just along for the ride, we were told. An exotic
dancer. She'd be returning to Inuvik with the pilots after they
dropped us off. Sure enough, she had her picture taken with

the Mould Bay airstrip sign, climbed back in, and we never
saw her again. We never spoke of her, either, her or the plane
that kept getting smaller in the sky until it disappeared.

The Lake and Her

muscles undulate, hair plasters into sand-patterns
water droplets chime the surface

fingernails leave white lines that turn pink
and don't hurt until you're dry

Four Short Poems: Fort McMurray

1.

a rutted mud road winds through
deer-coloured grass, fall
-stained brush
dark rotting logs, thin trunks
fire-blackened

I redden my fingertips
on iron oxide
from a broken stone

2.

cobalt clouds above
wet dark blue-grey clay

endless crumpled sky
            and
tattered stunted-tree horizon

stitched together
by ravens

3.

pee and melt snow
off a dark blue stone
giving it another day
or two of sky

4.

only light on
                  midnight
Greyhound bus

the redhead is braiding her hair

A World is Created

A green cloud, a spirit
that begins under the ground
and reaches to the sky,
and at the same time turns
back and reaches down again.

Billowing, a storm

with green raindrops.
With repetitions of fish
-shaped leaves in the wind,
the willow weeps
over the water.

Fire Wood

Between my hands
and the tree-hewn handle,
an animal's skin.
Between the handle and the log —
wood rushing towards wood —
a metal blade.

Trees sectioned and split:
that which was enclosed
exposed again to heat and light.

Gloves hung up to dry,
hands held up to warm,
steam from wet clothes
between me and the fire.
Me and these things between
the fire and our shadows.

Fire between you and me
and the night,
between where we sit and nowhere,
between us and nothing.

There is nothing
that cannot be found
between other things
between other things
between

Great Lakes Carp

The carp doesn't know
it's an invasive species.
It eats what it finds
in whatever water
it finds itself, Asian
or North American.

The carp has no way
of knowing that we've
decided it and all its kind
need to die; that now
we're just working
out the details.

The carp circles and dives,
feeds and breeds,
lives and dies. Breaks
the surface of the water
with its lips, as if
to kiss the moon.

Fire Meditations

. . . in the radical brackets of the embers and the stars . . .
— Max Oelschlaeger, *The Idea of Wilderness*

Dome tents, wigwams, igloos, kekulis
solidify the shape
a fire makes of the night.

A fire doesn't diminish the night
or the darkness; just helps us believe
they're smaller.

A fire is companionable,
an interesting conversationalist,
a good listener.

A fire is a magic mirror, colours
people across from you
the same flickering orange.

A fire keeps wild animals at bay
and keeps people warm;
smoke discourages biting insects.

A fire creates
as many shadows
as it frightens away.

A fire makes the night
even larger, turns
the campground into a cosmos:

close to a fire, we no longer
see the night sky; we
are seated around a star.

Long Lake Camp, Fort McMurray

four hundred thousand oil wells
in the province of Alberta alone
and at any given moment
one third of them are leaking

forty thousand people live
in camps just like this one
in and around Fort McMurray

there's a landscape
painting on the lunchroom wall but
it's of another place, not here

Ecotone, Site of Conflicting Desires

By way of preamble to our positive study of images of secrecy . . .
— Gaston Bachelard, *The Poetics of Space*

Among the stones beside
rivers down
pathways under
trees in
boxes up
stairs on
the shelves in dusty shops.

I've always walked sidewalks
as if they were beaches,
fragile strips of in-between
with the flow of traffic
or water on one side
and dry land, fixedness
on the other.

Land and water casting their changes:
broken wood and glass
in wave and sand:
smooth treasures.
Clam shells and seaweed
in sun and wind.
Windshields glitter in handfuls;
leaves and petals quicken asphalt.
Eventually, it is all worn down
into sand and dust.

Wardrobes with their
shelves, desks with their
drawers, and chests with their
false bottoms are veritable organs
of the secret psychological life.

Like us
through us
and for us
they have a quality of intimacy.

I walk the edge of melting snow,
the line between snow and earth,
between solid and liquid,
between winter and spring.
Freeze and thaw, night and day,

past and future, closed and open,
simile and metaphor, dark and light,
positive and imaginary,
memory and hope: without this edge
there is no place to walk.

Deer, City

if I were fluent in Whitetail
this what I would say:
You're going the wrong way!
Turn around, run back
until the roar is gone from your ears
until the lights stop hurting your eyes
until the ground is soft again
beneath your feet

Ed Rempel's Dog

Here's something, remember Ed Rempel's dog? Big German shepherd? Well, I was at the Hudson with Alvin earlier today and Ed comes in, pretty shaken up.

Turns out some of his chickens had taken to roosting in the hog barn, on the backs of the pigs. I don't know, maybe trying to stay warm? Anyways, come morning there were no more chickens. It's not like those pigs go hungry! They get all kinds of stuff on top of the regular feed. Small carrots from their garden, apple peels and cores from when Helen makes pies, you know. Ed practically spoils them. Anyways, bones and feathers and everything, the pigs ate them in the night. And those were some of his good laying hens.

So old Ed was pretty mad. So he goes to teach those pigs a lesson. Rocky, that's the German shepherd's name, he gets Rocky and puts him in the pig pen. Closed the door to the barn so there's nowhere for them to run. He said he was thinking, before he did it, "I hope Rocky don't hurt those pigs too bad," he just wanted to put a scare into them.

Then Ed had to drive down to Anderson's corner to pick something up, but he figured he wouldn't be longer than ten minutes. The pigs should still be okay in that little time. He was pretty mad though.

But when Ed gets back home, no Rocky! He thought maybe he'd jumped the fence and went back to the house, or the cow barn, but Ed couldn't find him anywhere. He said he walked through the pig-pen one more time and something caught his eye. A little patch of fur on the ground. It was Rocky's tail. Just his tail, that's all that was left! Can you believe that? That was a big dog. He had that dog for years, too. Ed was pretty shaken up.

Desire Lines

the years before the years we were
most consciously impressed
by the world, as if simply being
impressionable
meant the things we loved
the most must be displaced

think about the years lost
trying to find the years lost

childhood as an opening
door, horses
beckoning, warm earth,
cut cedar, soft rain

childhood as a desire
line traced in the sun
-flecked afternoon air
by the purring of a cat

Being Bee

bumble
bee, fall
ing drunk head
first into
blossoms
bee!
may you never
be sober

Bus Stop

it felt like the whole world
was shifting under his feet
but that was just the bus

and the smell of her hair
as she walked past

Water Dreams

When the ocean dreams about people
it's actually dreaming about sex.

Human beings, whether we believe
in a personal creation or an impersonal evolution,
can agree on one thing: it all began in the water.

In our work and art, in our bodies and dreams
we're drawn to the ocean.
To the tides, the ice, the foam, the waves.

Products of the imaginations of oceans,
we breathe water before we breathe air,
eat fish, cry and sweat salt, and build boats.

Whenever we laugh, or cry, or love, or remember,
the turtle-slumbering ocean is dreaming.

Apple

the hot red colour of its swaying
roundness that almost
begs for your fingertips
for the palm of your hand
for your mouth

the word in your mouth

the circle of it
the five-pointed star within
the circle made of mandorla
-seeds as deeply enclosed in
dark as your best secret

all of it beginning
and ending in mandala
blossoms, fragrant pale fleeting
as the tree-trunk axis mundi
is solid and old as the earth

Close

He had done a walk-around before he got into the truck.
Hit the horn three times before reversing.

The child's mother agreed that he was not at fault.

There is a legal document confirming his innocence.
Today, all these years later, does he still carry this piece of paper?

I imagine his rough fingers unfolding it,
him adjusting his bifocals to read.
I imagine the text, legal jargon or whatever it is,
not as text, and not as a tear-coloured blur, either,
but as a photograph of that young woman's face.
That day in the courthouse; her eyes.

A rare thing.

The only existing snapshot of her
that was not actually taken just
moments before she had to drive
home for the first time
without a daughter.

This is what he folds carefully and
returns to his breast pocket.

Spring

New leaves drawn across old feathers.
Trade your sleep for this music.
Not the songs of birds
but birds as the songs
of quickening sap.

Seeping through the hairline crack
in the morning's dark
unwinding.

"An Outburst of Wild Defiant Sorrow" (found)

Every living thing
(and perhaps many a dead one as well)
pays heed to that call.

To the deer it is a reminder
                    of the way of all flesh,
to the pine a forecast
                    of midnight scuffles and of blood upon the snow,
to the coyote a promise
                    of gleanings to come,
to the cowman a threat
                    of red ink at the bank,
to the hunter a challenge
                    of fang against bullet.

Yet behind these obvious
and immediate hopes and fears
there lies a deeper meaning, known only
to the mountain itself. Only the mountain has lived
long enough to listen objectively
to the howl of a wolf.

The Fort McMurray Trickster-Switch

There's old man coyote, he said,
gesturing with his cigarette.
Where's my rifle when I need it!

Then down the new dirt road
in the new white pickup
through the security gates, into camp.

Not hard to imagine a trickster here
having a laugh at our expense:
there are hundreds of us, from
as far away as Newfoundland,
staying in portable trailers,
in lumpy single bed small TV rooms,
loading into buses before dawn,
getting paid to build something
we don't understand for someone we don't know;
spending our days in snow and mud
in the bottoms of deep trenches.
But if so, the joke was on him.
Poor bastard; *deus otiosus*; trickster;
better he had conjured up a plague of locusts.

A week or two later
the coyote was back,
clay coloured and prairie-shadow thin
with cautious steps
on the newly excavated ground.
I'm sure he didn't recognize the place
we had been busy making into
the surface of the moon.

I thought I could feel him staring
but I couldn't look him in the eye.

We were held there for a moment,
orange-hardhat workers,
an invasive swarm of ants and trucks
and excavators as big as fossil
fuels turned back into dinosaurs.
So much noise and filth,
so much damage, the earth
herself sent someone to have a look.

Then the foreman threw a clump
of dirt at him, and he ran
back to the coyote-coloured earth.
I didn't see him again.

There was no other wildlife,
except ravens everywhere

shouting drunkenly,
labourers-back-in-camp-
after-the-peelers ravens;

big oily black
strutting executive
up-out-of-Calgary ravens.

Ravens jagged against the clouds,
ravens on dirt piles and idle equipment:
leave your shovel upright
and a raven would perch on it,
leave lunch unattended and
a raven would fly off with your sandwich.

There was another morning and another
seventh day. Another week, and another
in those lumpy bed trailers and those up-before-sunrise buses.
Twelve hours a day, boots in wet clay, using leather gloves
as seat cushions on the ice and icy metal,
drinking coffee barely warmer
and barely darker than coyote piss.

Benison

The hunter, alive to constant movements of nature, spirits, and human moods . . .

— Hugh Brody, *Maps and Dreams*

"Weather" is an oversimplification.
It's just a word. Like "animals."

Warm wind over the lake first thing
in the morning, mist wet and heavy
close to the ground, patches of sun
bright on snow between branches;

loud tail-slapping beaver or beaver
swimming, barely rippling the water,
old buck rubbing off its antlers, bear
finishing berries before going to sleep.

I dreamed a deer, and by this time next week
I'll be sending pieces of it by boat to my brothers.

Wolf Tree

The throat-pulse throb
of something not quite wind
from beneath the scalloped-feather wing
of magpie
am I.

The wolf tree split by lightning
behind you and the lightning flash in the basin
as you bend to wash your face

lightning in your hands cupped full of water

tree sentenced to stand burnt and alone

water to drink

charcoal to rub on your arms

your legs

for strength

am I.

Mothballing Mould Bay, NWT

This was my job: to operate the massive pump that shot the diesel fuel into the air, and the massive torch that ignited it. Behind this torch, which was like a piece of artillery, was a small portable trailer with side-by-side windows and matching easy chairs for two of us to sit in and watch the flame. This was my office.

Two guys on twelve-hour night shift, two guys on day. Not that night or day mattered because this far north in July it never got dark.

The torch needed constant attention: the diesel had to burn clean, and there were environmental consultants around to ensure that it did. If there was smoke, I tweaked the compressor just a little, enough to make the flame hotter. A thunderous twenty-foot jet of flame, twenty-four hours a day for two weeks straight. It was windy on the island, and we couldn't let the flame blow out.

Mould Bay is a joint Canada-U.S. Cold War-era weather station on Prince Patrick Island, in the Northwest Territories. Used to be staffed year-round by something like twenty people, but now a little computer or robot or something does all the work here that needs to be done.

When humans closed the place up, they didn't take much back with them. To this day the rec room still has a pool table and a piano. The library is still full of books. There are dormitories, kitchens, and workshops that look almost occupied. Slowly gathering polar desert dust. There are old vehicles parked here and there, and big military-green generators rusting outside. Once it was considered reasonable to bring these things up here by ship; now it would be far too expensive to think about bringing any of it back.

Our foreman was a grizzled old-timer who had been all over the North and brought with him a battered guitar and a bottle of spiced rum. He said to me, *You go ahead and take some of these books. They're just going to sit here and rot.*

See those big tanks? It would cost a lot more to ship all this diesel fuel out of here than it's actually worth. But we can't leave it here! Dangerous as hell that it's been sitting as long as it has. When these tanks rust through the spill will be incredible. We have to get rid of it.

We're going to burn it.

Vesica Piscis

I look to the bottom of the water,
not ignoring my reflection
or those of the dark trees
and clouds behind me,
but using them as a point of entry.

The smooth stones
on the stream bed
are stars.
I submerge
and try counting
but I can never hold
my breath long enough.
Rocks and pebbles,
sand and silt,
the stars recede
into unimaginable
distance.

The sky shifts
like water swelling
with spawning salmon.
The Milky Way is milt.
Constellations are egg
-laying patterns
in the night sky.

Mission Creek

with what must be a sigh of relief

with an open wound from tail to gill
showing white flesh beneath

the slow-moving and discoloured
Kokanee salmon just

stops fighting the current

Mould Bay Safety Meeting

loud noises won't scare em
so forget yr bells and whistles
never go out alone

but if one of em's after you, that's it
that's all she wrote
you just won't be able to run fast enough
even if you're on a four-wheeler
you might still be too slow

never go —

drop clothing behind
you as you run
it might get distracted
that'll buy you some time

never go out alone

On Your Knees, Biped

put your face into the fox's den, or is it a badger's?
a close fit, like putting on a mask,
with its strong musk air old dry fur wet dark garden
soil slowly alive with worms and root-tips:
become the earth and see through its eyes

Mourning Doves and Crows

The spirits of the cool morning air
before sunrise might be the same

as the tree spirits before the leaves turn gold.
The spirits are not the same

colour but both resemble shadow;
both have wings the colour of sleep.

Both fly out over the morning as if it is
an expanse of water and they are sent to find land.

One has a voice to jar you awake when you want
to rest; the other's is gentle and soothing but

you hear it in the morning instead of at night.
Although the spirits of dreams and forgetting

dreams and the spirits of sleep might sing
at the same time, they do not sing together.

But there are many who believe they do
or want it to be true the same way

they believe feathers belong to angels
and to fly is to deliver messages directly from God.

Fiat Lux

The most colourful life-forms
came into being alongside sense
-organs capable
of noticing them.

Wind-burned rock grew soil,
moss, grasses. Flowers and
insects bloomed
one another.

Light-sensitivity became vision.
Six hundred million years ago
the earth began
to see itself.

The First Metaphor (found)

I used to have a cat, an old fighting tom,
        The first
who would jump through the open window
        subject matter
by my bed in the middle of the night
        for painting
and land on my chest. I'd half-awaken.
        was animal.
He'd stick his skull under my nose and purr,
        Probably
stinking of urine and blood.
        the first paint
Some nights he kneaded my bare chest
        was animal blood.
with his front paws, powerfully, arching
        Prior to that,
his back, as if sharpening his claws,
        it is not unreasonable
or pummeling a mother for milk.
        to suppose that
And some mornings I'd wake in daylight to find
        the first metaphor
my body covered with paw prints in blood;
        was animal.
I looked as though I'd been painted with roses.

Stories

The one where the protagonist wishes
he could fly like a bird so he climbs to the top of
a tree and jumps. Or maybe he fashions wings
out of feathers and wax, but either way he flies

to pieces when he smashes into the ground.
These are stories, or they might be, meant
to warn us about the danger of extremes.
Look, he gave it a shot, and see where it got him.

Acts of great passion or great recklessness.
The one where the protagonist tries
to love everyone
and he teaches people to forgive their enemies

or does he tell them the truth they seek
can be found within?
Regardless, he doesn't get too far: people do
the opposite of what he proposes, and kill him.

Surprisingly, these stories almost always end
well. Broken bodies are reassembled. Life restored.
And finally, eventually, someone sees the new
person or maybe the old person with new eyes.

Another One

For every conversation among immigrants
who speak in a language he doesn't understand,
who he believes might be talking about him,
a different vein stands out on his forehead.

For you young people who stare, or ignore him,
or have done some god-awful thing with your hair,
or have rings in your lips or noses,
a twinge, another dull ache in his lower back.

For every recollection of her face, her smile, her skin,
her warm eyes on him,
and for every day he wakes up
and rides the bus downtown without her,

for every word he didn't say to her when he could have,
every word he didn't even think about
until years passed,
another one, and another.

Poem in the Middle of Nowhere

This is a prairie road.
The road is the shortest distance
between nowhere and nowhere.
This road is a poem.

— Robert Kroetsch, *Seed Catalogue*

In the middle of prairie winter
open spaces and ice

blown tire, exploded ballpoint,
snow-blindness from the empty page.

Gravel for traction and stability:
words and smudges of ink.

We do this to soothe the eyes
and to stay between the lines
away from the ditch and the emptiness.

Walking Path

Starlight prisms
through atmosphere
and lies with the earth.

Spirit and matter
eat and drink and breathe
each other in and out,

condense into sunspots
of marmot fur and nuthatch feathers,
gopher snake scales and deer mouse bones,

planets with appetites
and snowberry
constellations.

Shift

The snap of a twig underfoot:
just enough time to witness
a grebe's easy dive into lakewater,
or a duck's lift from the surface into flight.

Enough to see how it might be done:
the shift from element to element.

The snap of a twig underfoot.
What is a human being?
Jealous?
Lonely?

Bear Being

I can think better about the bear this way
with my feet in the cold creek, the sun on my back,
my teeth dark with chokecherries.

I see no salmon but dream about flipping them
out of the water, biting into one still slapping on the rocks.

If I am a bear, does the sound of the creek soothe me?
Am I irritated by or alarmed by distant traffic?
Or do both these sounds belong to the same world?

I smell a wet dog but it and the other one,
the tall one, are heading in the other direction.

I'm hungry and I remember
the big grasshoppers beside the trail.

Water that felt cold on my feet, at first,
now feels warm. Do I think about these things?

To what extent does a bear contrast this moment
with ten minutes ago, the present with the past?

I smell nothing but marshy water
and hear only flowing sounds.

I become so still and quiet a passing hunter
might lower his spear or bow or rifle
and learn how to sit the way I am sitting.

This, he might realize, will make him a better hunter.
Of course I do not think about these things.

My mind wanders back to the patch of chokecherries.
Then I smell the hunter and turn to run
too late; my mouth fills up with blood.

Basin

Warmest it's been
all spring, the doctor said.
I didn't expect to see
this today. My feet
the colour of that evening
on the mountain, stars
cool drops of water
burning the dark
blue frost
-bitten sky.

Sites

1.

I could have caught it if I had moved a little quicker, but the ground was pure mud: a baby jackrabbit the size of a leather work glove huddled under a wooden walkway. I wondered where its mother was; if we had excavated its warren or filled it with cement; if we had frightened off or killed its family. I'd have taken the baby rabbit home, tried to keep it alive, but it was too fast. Tiny, alone, and with nowhere to run but the construction site. Still, it was wild enough to run.

2.

A new subdivision where just one year before there had been only canola fields and wetlands. We were loading used wooden walkways into the back of the truck when a shadow drew our eyes upward. A cloudless day, a dazzling blue sky, and one big white pelican circling. We may have been standing on the site of the pond where this bird had rested every year on its way north; whoever moves into this neighbourhood, whoever eventually calls this spot of ground their backyard, will never know.

We ate lunch in the truck so we wouldn't have to watch that endless circling.

Notes

Page 22, "Ritual: To Find Out How Much Sunlight is Left" Coward, Garth and Paul Presidente. *Wilderness Survival.* Victoria: Information Division, British Columbia Forest Service, 1976 (pages 44-45).

Page 26, "The Omnivore's Dilemma" Henry David Thoreau, Walden, cited in *Oelschlaeger 1991* (161-162).

Page 29 "The Human Skin" Snyder, Gary. "Writers and the War Against Nature" in *Back on the Fire: Essays.* Berkeley: Counterpoint Press, 2007 (69).

Page 52, "Ecotone, Site of Conflicting Desires" Bachelard, Gaston. *The Poetics of Space. Boston: Beacon Press*, 1969 (78).

Page 63, "An Outburst of Wild Defiant Sorrow" Aldo Leopold, "Thinking Like a Mountain" cited in *Murray*, 1993 (21).

Page 76, "The First Metaphor" Dillard, Annie. *Pilgrim at Tinker Creek.* New York: Harper & Row, 1974 (1).
Berger, John. *Why Look at Animals?* New York: Penguin Books, 2009 (16).

Acknowledgements

This collection began as a Creative Writing MFA thesis at UBC Okanagan, in Kelowna British Columbia. There I had the privilege of working with Nancy Holmes, whose insight and enthusiasm made this book possible.

For their poetry classes and conversations, and for their expertise and generosity, I would like to thank John Lent, Michael Kenyon, Sharon Thesen, Sonnet L'Abbé, Michael V. Smith, Emily Nilsen, Don McKay, and Harold Rhenisch. Thank you also to all the writers, workers, scholars, artists, travelers, and teachers — in the Okanagan, Edmonton, and elsewhere — I have had the pleasure of knowing.

I am grateful to Thistledown Press for giving these poems a home.

This research and writing was funded in part by a Graduate Entrance Scholarship, and by two University Graduate Fellowship awards, at UBC Okanagan.

I would also like to acknowledge that this book was written on unceded Syilx land.

Finally, thank you to Karen for your gift of endless patience and support.

Earlier versions of the following poems have been published:

"Ed Rempel's Dog" and "Mould Bay NWT Safety Meeting" — in *OK Magpie*, Vol. 2, Spring 2015, Kelowna BC.

"Odd" — Irish language version on *Rogha Gabriel*, Gabriel Rosenstock's poetry blog, 2014. http://roghaghabriel.blogspot.ca/2014/08/corr.html

"Webs Across the Eyes", "Odd", "The First Metaphor", "*Agelaius phoeniceus*", "An Outburst of Wild Defiant Sorrow", "Water Dreams", "Wolf Tree", "Mourning Doves and Crows", "Walking Path", "Shift", and "Bear Being" — with linocuts by Alison

Kubbos, in the gallery exhibition and chapbook *The First Metaphor* (The Bleeding Heart Artspace, Edmonton Poetry Festival 2015; Gallery Vertigo, Vernon BC, summer 2014).

"Honing", "Four Short Poems: Fort McMurray", "Long Lake Camp, Fort McMurray", "Close", "The Fort McMurray Trickster-Switch", and "Sites" — in the chapbook *Fort McMurray Tricksters*, Alfred Gustav Press, Vancouver. Winter 2014.

"Fire" and "Shift" — in *Elephant Mountain*, No, 1, 2013/2014.

"On Your Knees, Biped" — in *Lake: Journal of Arts and Environment*. http://www.lakejournal.ca/soundings_poems.html

"The Straight Lines of Cities" — in *Jones Av.*, XVI/1 Summer 2011.